Sushi Recipe

By Brad Hoskinson

Table of Contents

Aunt Keiko's Inarisushi

Aunt Keiko's Inarisushi is a delicious dish tantalizing your taste buds. This popular Japanese dish is made with rice and vegetables wrapped in fried tofu skin. The dish is then simmered in a sweet vinegar sauce. Aunt Keiko's Inarisushi is sure to please even the most discerning palate.

Prep Time 10 mins | Cook Time 35 mins | Total Time 45 mins

Ingredients

- ✓ 650 g Sushi rice
- ✓ 7 abura age cut them in half and make 12
- ✓ 260 ml water
- ✓ 2 tsp dashi powder
- ✓ 35 g sugar
- ✓ 1 tsp miso paste
- ✓ 30 ml soy sauce
- ✓ 1 tbsp black sesame seeds to sprinkle

Instructions

1. Cook and prepare the sushi rice (my sushi rice uses 2 cups of uncooked rice and I used about 1 of the entire cooked rice) *1
2. Cut the aburaage pieces in half.
3. Pour boiling hot water over the aburaage to remove the excess oil.
4. Bring one cup of water in a saucepan to boil over high heat and add dashi powder.
5. Add sugar and soy sauce to the saucepan.
6. Turn the heat down to medium, add aburaage and cook for 15 minutes.
7. Add miso paste and cook until all liquid has absorbed and evaporated.

8. Turn the heat off and cool it down completely.

9. Make 15 round and cylinder shape sushi rice balls (each weighing about 55 g)

10. Keep one sushi rice ball in a secure location away from harm and open the end toward the direction it was previously closed.

11. Repeat this same process for the rest of the 12 aburaage and rice balls.

12. Serve on a plate and sprinkle black sesame seeds on top.

Smoked Salmon Sushi Roll-Ups with Citrus Soy Sauce

This dish is an easy and impressive appetizer that is perfect for a party. Smoked salmon sushi roll-ups with citrus soy sauce are healthy, flavorful, and beautiful. They can be made ahead of time and stored in the refrigerator until you're ready to serve them. Your guests will be impressed with your culinary skills!

Prep Time 20 mins | Total Time 20 mins

Ingredients

For the salmon rolls:

- ✓ 9 oz smoked Salmon
- ✓ 1 cup whipped cream cheese
- ✓ 3 Tbsp green onion, finely chopped
- ✓ 3 tsp lemon zest
- ✓ 2 tsp lemon juice
- ✓ 2/3 of a cucumber, sliced into thin strips
- ✓ 1 of an avocado, cut into thin strips
- ✓ 2 Tbsp everything but the bagel seasoning (EBTB)

For the citrus soy sauce:

- ✓ 3 Tbsp soy sauce
- ✓ 3 Tbsp lemon juice
- ✓ 2 Tbsp water
- ✓ 2 tsp mirin
- ✓ 2 Tbsp green onion, sliced thin

Instructions

To make the soy sauce:

Stir the sauce ingredients in a small bowl and place them in the fridge while preparing your salmon rolls.

To make the salmon rolls:

1. Spread out a large piece of plastic wrap on your countertop and put some EBTB seasoning on it. Sprinkle your smoked salmon over the seasoning until a 4-by-4 rectangle is formed. (Make sure that your slices overlap slightly.)

2. Next, mix your cream cheese, green onion, lemon juice, and lemon zest together and spread it over the Salmon. Then place your sliced avocado and cucumber strips in the center of the rectangle. Very carefully, use the plastic wrap to help roll the Salmon over your avocado and cucumber and continue rolling until you reach the other side. Place your salmon roll in the freezer for 15-20 minutes to firm up slightly. (This makes it much easier to cut!)

3. When ready, take the roll out of the freezer, slice it and serve immediately with your soy sauce.

Keto Shrimp California Sushi Roll

Sushi is a delicious, traditional Japanese dish that can be enjoyed in many different ways. One popular variation is the Keto Shrimp California Sushi Roll. This version of sushi uses shrimp as the main protein wrapped in nori (seaweed) and rice. It is then rolled up and served with soy sauce and wasabi.

Prep Time 35 mins | Cook Time 0 mins | Total Time 35 mins

Ingredients

- ✓ Shrimp California Sushi
- ✓ 2 Cucumbers (seedless) very thinly sliced lengthwise
- ✓ 3/8 Red bell pepper finely chopped
- ✓ 3/8 Red bell pepper cut into small pieces
- ✓ 4 ounces shrimp cooked and finely chopped
- ✓ 4 ounces shrimp cooked and cut into small pieces
- ✓ 1 Avocado cut into small pieces
- ✓ 2 teaspoons Lime juice
- ✓ 7 ounces Cream cheese softened
- ✓ 3 tablespoons fresh dill, chopped
- ✓ 3 tablespoons Sesame seeds toasted
- ✓ 20 Capers Goya are Gluten free

Dipping Sauce

- ✓ 1 teaspoon Wasabi
- ✓ 4 tablespoons Coconut aminos

Instructions

Shrimp California Sushi

1. Use a Mandoline to slice the cucumber lengthwise a bit smaller than 1/8 inch thick. You will need 18 thin strips. Place on a paper towel and press a few times with another paper towel to reduce the water content. Set aside.

2. Chop the red bell pepper into small pieces and approximately 3 ounces of cooked shrimp (use a food chopper). Then cut the rest of the shrimp, red pepper, and avocado into small pieces (about 1/4 inch). You want a distinct piece of shrimp, red pepper, and avocado for each roll. Drizzle lime juice over the avocado and set aside.

3. In a small bowl, combine the softened cream cheese with the finely chopped red pepper pieces and shrimp.

4. Lay all of the cucumber slices on top of the toasted sesame seeds before rolling. Press down slightly so the seeds will stick to the cucumber. Start at one end and spread the cream cheese mixture the length of the cucumber. Add the larger pieces of shrimp, red pepper, and avocado on top of the cream cheese mixture. Roll tightly from the end. The cream cheese on end should seal the outer edge and the toasted sesame seeds should be visible outside each roll.

5. Place a caper or two on top of each roll and a small amount of dill.

6. Refrigerate for 15 minutes, then serve cold. Serve with wasabi paste and soy sauce for dipping.

Dipping Sauce

Combine a very small amount of the plated wasabi with the coconut aminos in a small server ramekin and stir - taste for heat.

Giant Sushi Cake

A sushi cake is a type of sushi that is shaped like a cake. It is made by layering sushi rice, seafood, and vegetables on top of each other and then pressing them together into a mold. Sushi cakes can be decorated with fish, Shells, and other seafood.

Serves 9

Ingredients

For the sushi rice:

- ✓ 4 cups Spekko Royal Umbrella Jasmine Rice
- ✓ 2 tsp salt
- ✓ 3/4 cup rice vinegar
- ✓ 2 tbsp sugar

For the filling:

- ✓ 6 tins (190g each) of shredded tuna
- ✓ 2 cups mayonnaise
- ✓ 2 cucumbers, sliced thinly into rounds
- ✓ 3 avocados, sliced thinly

Serving suggestion:

- ✓ 2 tubs (270g) of cream cheese
- ✓ 2 cups black sesame seeds (optional)
- ✓ 2 avocados, sliced and arranged into roses
- ✓ 2 cups pickled ginger, drained and rolled into roses
- ✓ 2 cucumbers, peeled into ribbons and rolled into roses
- ✓ 2 cups sushi mayonnaise
- ✓ 2 cups soya sauce

Instructions

Line the base and sides of a springform cake tin with clingfilm.

For the sushi rice:

1. Rinse the rice thoroughly under cold water until the water runs clear.

2. Combine the rice and 1 tsp salt in a pot and cover with 3 cups of cold water. Soak for 35 minutes. Cover with a lid, bring to a boil and simmer for 20-25 minutes, or until the water has been absorbed. Remove from the heat, place a kitchen towel in between the pot and lid and allow to stand for 15 minutes. Spread the steamed rice over a baking tray to cool.

3. Combine rice vinegar, brown sugar, and salt in a small saucepan. Bring to a simmer over medium heat, stirring until the sugar is dissolved. Remove the pan from the heat, and allow the ingredients to cool.

4. Stir the vinegar mixture through the cooled rice and set aside.

To assemble:

1. Divide the rice into 3 equal portions.

2. Press 1 portion into the bottom of the springform cake tin. Ensure it is compact, smooth and level.

3. Combine the tuna with the mayonnaise and spread a thin layer over the rice. Add a layer of cucumber slices, followed by avocado slices.

4. Repeat the layers of rice, tuna mayonnaise, cucumber, and avocado one more time, ending with a third layer of rice.

5. Place clingfilm over the cake's top to avoid drying out, then place in the fridge for at least an hour.

6. Carefully remove the cake from the springform and set it on a flat, level plate or cake stand.

7. Using a knife, cover the entire cake with a thin layer of cream cheese.

8. Press handfuls of black sesame seeds onto the tops and sides of the cake, ensuring the whole is entirely covered.

9. Pipe layers of mayonnaise onto the cake and garnish with avocado flowers, pickled ginger flowers, and cucumber ribbon flowers using a piping bag and nozzle.

10. Slice generous portions and ENJOY!

Tuna Sushi Rolls

You'll love this easy recipe for tuna sushi rolls if you're a sushi lover. They're healthy, delicious, and perfect for a quick lunch or dinner. Best of all, they only take a few minutes to make. So what are you waiting for? Give them a try!

Prep Time 20 mins | Total Time 20 mins

Ingredients

- ✓ 2 cups cooked sushi rice
- ✓ 3-4 tablespoons seasoned rice vinegar
- ✓ 3 sheets nori
- ✓ 6 ounces tuna in water
- ✓ 1 cucumber, cut into strips
- ✓ 1 avocado, cut lengthwise

Instructions

1. Prep the nori. Lay nori, shiny side down, on a sushi mat or plastic wrap 3 sheets of nori

2. Blend the rice and vinegar. Mix seasoned rice vinegar into the sushi rice using a sideways chopping motion.

   2 cups cooked sushi rice, 3-7 tablespoons seasoned rice vinegar

3. Spread 1 cup of the rice mixture onto the nori sheets, leaving a few spaces on one end without any rice. Top each bread roll with a horizontal line of cucumber, avocado, and tuna. Roll the nori on top of each of these ingredients.

   1 cucumber, cut into strips,1 avocado, cut lengthwise,6 ounces tuna in water

4. Seal the roll, then slice. Dip your fingers in water, run them along the top portion of the nori, and finish rolling. The water seals the roll, keeping it wrapped together. Using a sharp knife, slice the roll in half, then into thirds.

BLT Sushi

Anyone who loves sushi and bacon will go crazy for this BLT Sushi. It's the perfect combination of two of everyone's favorite things. This dish is so easy to make and only requires a few ingredients. You'll be sure to impress your friends and family with this unique twist on a classic dish.

PREP TIME: 15 MINS | COOK TIME: 25 MINS | TOTAL TIME: 55 MINS

Ingredients

- ✓ 12 slices bacon
- ✓ 3 tbsp. mayonnaise
- ✓ 2 c. chopped tomatoes
- ✓ 1 avocado, diced
- ✓ 2 c. shredded romaine
- ✓ Kosher salt
- ✓ Freshly ground black pepper

Directions

1. Preheat the oven to 420° and place a wire rack over a large baking sheet. Place 5 slices of bacon side by side. Lift one end of every other bacon slice and place another bacon slice on top of the lifted pieces. Lay slices back. Next, lift opposite bacon slices back and place a bacon slice on top. Lay slices back down. Repeat the weaving process until you have a bacon weave of 5 strips by 6 strips. Set bacon weave on prepared baking sheet.

2. Bake until bacon is cooked but still pliable, 25 minutes.

3. Pat bacon weave with paper towels to drain fat and transfer to a piece of plastic wrap (it helps with rolling!)

4. Slice bacon into small pieces and lay them on the slice of bread. Top the bacon with slices of vegetables and sprinkle on paprika. Sprinkle with mayonnaise and place the sandwich in the toaster oven. Season to taste with pepper.

5. Starting from the bottom, tightly roll, then slice crosswise into "sushi rolls."

Crazy Mango Sushi Roll

You'll go crazy for this delicious mango sushi roll if you love sushi and mangos! This easy recipe only requires a few ingredients, and it's the perfect way to enjoy the sweet taste of mangos with the savory flavors of sushi.

Prep Time 15 minutes | Total Time 15 minutes

Ingredients

- ✓ 2 ripe mangoes
- ✓ 5 tempuras shrimp
- ✓ 3/4 Hass avocado
- ✓ 3 cups cooked & seasoned sushi rice
- ✓ 3 nori

Instructions

1. Prepare tempura shrimp. Follow my guide if you don't know how to make Japanese tempura shrimp.

2. Cut avocado into long strips.

3. Roll avocado strips and tempura shrimp with rice and nori using uramaki style.

4. Use a mandoline, peeler, or sharp knife to slice the mango into thin, long slices.

5. Have two plastic wraps (the size of a rolling mat) ready on a flat surface.

6. Arrange mango slices onto plastic wrap to fill a rectangular area of about 7" x 2".

7. Place inside-out sushi roll directly on top of mango slices.

8. Now roll while lifting plastic wrap to cover; your rolls should have a nice layer of mango cover.

9. Keep the plastic on until cutting for better shape; repeat for the next roll.

10. When ready to serve, use a sharp knife to cut, then gently unroll each piece out of the plastic wrap.

11. Drizzle some mango sauce and serve immediately.

Sweet Potato Sushi Rolls

Sushi is a delicious Japanese dish that can be made with a variety of different ingredients. Sweet potatoes are an excellent option for sushi rolls because they are sweet and savory and add a unique flavor to the dish. These sweet potato sushi rolls are easy to make and will be a hit with your friends and family.

PREP TIME 25 mins | COOK TIME 35 mins | TOTAL TIME 60 mins

Ingredients

For The Sushi Rice

- ✓ 2 cups short grain brown rice - or choose a classic Japanese white sushi rice
- ✓ 3 tbsp rice vinegar
- ✓ 2 tbsp maple syrup or agave nectar
- ✓ 1 tsp salt

For The Crispy Sweet Potato

- ✓ 1 cup white whole wheat flour - or brown rice flour for a gluten-free recipe
- ✓ 1 cup water
- ✓ 3 cups panko - choose gluten-free panko if needed
- ✓ 1 tsp garlic powder
- ✓ 1 tsp salt
- ✓ 2 large sweet potatoes - peeled and sliced into long sticks of about 1 1/2 inches thick.

For The Roll

- ✓ nori sheets
- ✓ cucumber - julienned
- ✓ avocado - sliced

For Serving (Optional)

- ✓ soy sauce - or tamari for a gluten-free option
- ✓ spicy Mayo - see notes
- ✓ sesame seeds
- ✓ wasabi
- ✓ pickled ginger

Instructions

Make The Sushi Rice

Start by cooking the sushi rice accordingly to the packaging instructions. Once cooked, add the rice vinegar, maple syrup, and salt and gently stir to combine. Set aside so the rice can cool down.

Make The Crispy Sweet Potato

1. Preheat the oven to 420°. Line a baking sheet with parchment paper.

2. In a medium bowl, add the flour + water and stir to combine until there are no clumps anymore. It should be a thick batter. Mix the panko, garlic powder, and salt in a second medium bowl.

3. Then, taking one stick of sweet potato at a time, dip into the batter covering all surfaces, then hit the side of the bowl to remove the excess before transferring to the bowl with the panko. Then, using your hands, cover and press gently on the sweet potato so the panko sticks to its surface. When completely covered, then transfer to the baking sheet. Keep going until you are done with all of the sweet potato pieces.

4. Bake in the oven for 35 minutes, flipping halfway through.

Roll The Sushi

1. Lay the sushi mat on the surface, then cover it with a nori sheet (on the rough side facing up). Then, use your fingers to cover the nori sheet with the rice (not too thick), spreading it evenly on all its

surface while leaving 3-4 inches free of rice on top. You can wet your hands slightly if the rice sticks.

2. Then, leave about 3 inches free of filling at the bottom and add the breaded sweet potato, cucumber, and avocado slices (see pictures in the blog and video). Then, lift the bottom of the mat with your thumbs while holding the filling with your fingers and start rolling while tucking the stuffing inside the roll. When you get to the top, wet the surface that's free of rice and then finish the rolling. Gently press to help seal the roll and shape it.

3. Use a sharp knife to cut the roll into maki (wet the blade to prevent the rice from sticking to it if needed).

4. Drizzle a spicy mayo, sprinkle sesame seeds over the maki, and serve with soy sauce, pickled ginger, and wasabi, if desired.

Crispy Rice Sushi with Smoked Salmon Bang Bang Sauce

This dish is a fun and easy way to enjoy sushi without all the fuss. The rice is crispy and the Salmon is smoked, giving it a delicious flavor. The Bang Bang sauce is a perfect finishing touch.

Prep Time 35 minutes | Cook Time 25 minutes | Total Time 60 minutes

Ingredients

For the rice:

- ✓ 8.74 oz short grain white rice, often labeled as "sushi rice."
- ✓ 3 tbsp coconut aminos
- ✓ 2 tbsp rice vinegar
- ✓ 3 tsp toasted sesame oil
- ✓ Avocado oil or avocado oil spray

For the topping:

- ✓ 3 whole mini-Persian cucumbers thinly slice into rounds
- ✓ 2-3 whole avocados sliced into small pieces
- ✓ 3 oz. smoked Salmon
- ✓ Chive chopped
- ✓ Furikake or toasted sesame seeds, optional

Bang Bang Sauce

- ✓ 1 cup mayonnaise
- ✓ 4 tbsp rice vinegar
- ✓ 1-2 tsp hot sauce. I use Frank's original
- ✓ 0.3 oz Garlic grated or crushed, about 1 large clove
- ✓ 2 tbsp coconut aminos

✓ 2 tbsp ketchup

✓ 3 pinches of coarse sea salt

Instructions

A night before:

1. Follow the instructions that come with the rice package. Once the rice has reached the correct temperature, mix it with sesame oil, rice vinegar, and coconut aminos.

2. Line, a generous-sized single layer of food, cling wrap inside an 8" by 8" (20 cm) square-shaped baking dish or a container with a flat bottom. This will be the mold to shape the sushi block.

3. Add the rice to the container. Compress it down and flatten it tightly using a rice paddle or the back of a spoon to help the rice grains stick together. Press it down tight and shape it as flat and even as possible. Focus particularly around the corners and the edge, as these are the areas where the rice tends to fall apart. The height of the rice block should roughly be around 3/4 -inch (2 cm) thick.

4. You can also make use of the container liner to help you reshape the edge of the rice by gently shifting it upward and having it sink inward to help you cluster grains.

5. Once the rice grains are compressed into a big block and once it's cool to room temperature. Seal the container and refrigerate overnight.

Serving day:

1. Wet the chopping board with water so the rice won't stick to the board. Carefully lift the rice block out of the container and remove the cling wrap. Slice the rice block into roughly 11 rectangular-shaped and equal-sized pieces. You can dip the knife in a bowl of water to help slice.

2. To Air Fry: Preheat your air fryer. Spray the fryer basket with avocado oil. Spray the rice sushi pieces with another thin layer of oil, then place the oiled side into the basket. Leave some space

between the pieces. Air fry at 390F (195C) for 10 minutes. Spray another thin layer of oil and carefully flip them to air fry for another 8 additional minutes. The rice sushi should come out golden and a little crispy. Cool them down over a baking rack.

3. To pan fry: Preheat a frying skillet over medium heat until it feels warm. Add 4-5 tbsp avocado oil. Add the rice sushi pieces. Leave some space between each piece. You should hear the sizzling sound. Pan fry for 4 minutes or until you see the bottom turns golden brown, then flip to cook another 5-6 minutes. Add more oil if needed. The texture should be crispy golden outside, soft, and a chewy little inside. Cool them down over a baking rack

To serve:

Place your rice sushi with a thin moat of avocado, cucumbers, and smoked salmon on top. Drizzle with the bang bang sauce and sprinkle with chives and furikake, if using. Then, serve.

Spicy Shrimp Sushi Stacks

If you love sushi but are looking for something different, then you'll love these Spicy Shrimp Sushi Stacks. They're easy to make and full of flavor. Plus, they look impressive, so your guests will be impressed.

Prep Time: 15 minutes | Cook Time: 25 minutes | Total Time: 40 minutes

Ingredients

For the sushi rice:

- ✓ 2 cups uncooked short-grained rice, well rinsed
- ✓ 3 cups water
- ✓ 3 tablespoons rice vinegar
- ✓ 2 tablespoons sugar
- ✓ 2 teaspoons salt

For the avocado and cucumber layer:

- ✓ 2 cups avocado, mashed
- ✓ 2 cups cucumber, diced
- ✓ 2 tablespoons lime juice
- ✓ salt to taste

For the spicy Shrimp:

- ✓ 1 pound cooked shrimp, diced
- ✓ 4 tablespoons mayonnaise
- ✓ 2 tablespoons sriracha

For the stacks:

- ✓ 5 teaspoons furikake

Instructions

For the sushi rice:

1. Pour in the rice and water, bring to a boil, reduce the heat, and simmer, covered, until the rice is tender and the water has been absorbed, about 25 minutes. Let it cool slightly before consuming.

2. Gently fold the mixture of the rice vinegar, sugar, and salt into the rice.

    For the avocado and cucumber layer:

3. Mix everything.

For the spicy shrimp:

4. Mix everything.

For the stacks:

5. Place the rice into the stack guides, pat down lightly, and top with the avocado and cucumber mixture, followed by the shrimp mixture and a sprinkle of furikake.

Recipe For Volcano Sushi Roll

Volcano sushi roll is a type of sushi that is made with a special kind of rice. The rice is mixed with vinegar, sugar, and salt and then rolled into a ball. The ball is placed on top of a piece of nori and then topped with fish or vegetables. The sushi is then rolled up and served with soy sauce and wasabi.

Prep Time 20 minutes | Cook Time 15 minutes

Ingredients

Sushi roll

- ✓ 3 sheets nori
- ✓ 2 cups cooked & seasoned sushi rice
- ✓ 5 sticks kani - imitation crab
- ✓ 0.7 mini cucumber

Spicy Mayo

- ✓ 0.7 Tbsp Sriracha adjust to spicy tolerant
- ✓ 5 Tbsp Kewpie mayo or regular Mayo

Lava topping

- ✓ 14 prawn or equivalent substitution
- ✓ 15 mini scallop
- ✓ 2 Tbsp cream cheese optional
- ✓ 4 Tbsp spicy mayo

Garnish & Decoration

- ✓ 2 Tbsp Masago flying roe
- ✓ 2 Tbsp unagi sauce

Instructions

Spicy mayo sauce

1. Mix 5 level spoons of Mayo (or 4 heaps) in a mixing bowl with half Tbsp of Sriracha. Adjust the amount of Sriracha to your spicy-tolerant level.

2. After mixing it well, set it aside to rest for a couple minutes. The sauce will turn out a nice yellow color and be ready for any glazing.

Lava Topping

1. Preheat oven to 420 F

2. Cut kani sticks into 3 or 4, and add to the mixing container.

3. Mince half of the shrimp and finely mince the rest. This is to preserve some variation in the final texture.

4. Slice and dice scallops if they're too big.

5. Add cream cheese and a spoon of spicy mayo sauce. Or replace cream cheese with extra spicy Mayo.

6. Add some drops of lemon juice if you like the flavor.

7. Use a fork to mix while breaking kani sticks into thin strips. Mix them well.

8. Level and spread some extra spicy mayo all over the top surface.

9. Bake for 14-17 minutes or until it's bubbling and the shrimp are done.

Rolling sushi base

1. Lay a piece of nori, shiny side down, on top of the rolling mat over a flat surface.

2. Spread cooked and seasoned sushi rice atop nori and apply some pressure with your fingers tips.

3. Add kani and cucumber strips or your favorite fillings.

4. Lift the mat and roll while applying pressure gently to form a shape.

5. Cover with plastic wrap and set aside till ready to assemble/serve. Repeat for other rolls if needed.

Assembling

1. Cut each sushi roll into slices; the thinner slice is preferred due to the extra height from the volcano topping (13-15 pieces/rolls instead of the regular 8).

2. Arrange them all on serving plates.

3. For each slice, carefully spoon on the lava shrimp mixture.

4. Drizzle extra spicy mayo and unagi sauce all over the pieces.

5. Top off with some masago or a dot of Sriracha for an even spicier taste.

6. Serve immediately. No soy sauce is needed as the overall flavor should be quite balanced a bit of everything.

Spicy Crab Roll | Kani Maki

A kani maki, or crab roll, is a type of sushi made with crab meat and cucumber. It is a popular dish in Japanese cuisine and can be found at most sushi restaurants. The crab meat is usually mixed with mayonnaise and rice vinegar, which gives it a slightly sweet and tangy flavor. The cucumber provides a refreshing crunch to the roll, while the nori seaweed wrapper gives it a savory umami flavor.

Prep Time: 35 minutes | Cook Time: 25 minutes | Total Time: 60 minutes

Ingredients

Sushi Rice

- ✓ 2 cups Japanese short grain rice
- ✓ 2 cups cold water
- ✓ 4 tbsp sushi rice vinegar

Sushi Roll

- ✓ 3 pcs avocado sliced into strips
- ✓ 2 pc cucumber sliced into strips
- ✓ 270 g crab sticks (kani) cut into half lengthwise
- ✓ 2 pc seaweed nori sheet
- ✓ masago orange fish roe
- ✓ sriracha chili sauce
- ✓ kewpie mayonnaise
- ✓ gomashio sesame seed seasoning

Instructions

1. Cook the sushi rice. Once cooked, mix in the sushi vinegar. Leave it to cool to room temperature.

2. Mix sriracha sauce and mayonnaise together in a bowl. After shredding the crab meat, add the sriracha mayo and mix it well. Toast the nori sheet.

3. Place a sheet of cling plastic wrap on a flat surface, then place a sushi bamboo mat on it. Use a knife to cut through a sheet of seaweed into two portions, and spread seaweed with a rice sponge. Press the lower portion of the rice sponge on a flat surface, then sprinkle gomashio on it.

4. Now, flip the rice and nori sheet, so your seaweed faces up. You can add the spicy Kani salad in Step 2 to the middle of the nori sheet. Add the avocado, cucumber, and mango on top of it, with some mayonnaise.

5. Roll the bamboo mat starting at the edge with both hands, pressing it down firmly, and continue until you reach the end. Leave in the fridge for at least 70 minutes or in the freezer for only 20 minutes. You can now cut your kani maki into pieces and remove the cling wrap for serving.

6. If you'd like, you may place your masago on a plate, then roll each sushi slice onto the masago. Now you are ready to serve your spicy crab roll!

Shrimp Tempura Sushi Recipe

A delicious shrimp tempura sushi recipe is perfect for a quick and easy meal. This dish can be made in under 30 minutes and is packed with flavors. The shrimp is coated in a light tempura batter and then fried until golden brown. It is then rolled up in sushi rice and nori seaweed. Serve with soy sauce, pickled ginger, and wasabi for a complete meal.

PREP TIME 20 mins | COOK TIME 10 mins

Ingredients

Shrimp Tempura Sushi Roll

- ✓ 2 lb Tempura Shrimp store-bought - baked according to instructions
- ✓ 2 English cucumbers thinly sliced into julienned pieces
- ✓ 3 large avocados sliced
- ✓ 5 sheets Nori
- ✓ 3 tablespoons tobiko for garnish
- ✓ Unagi Sushi Sauce optional

Sushi Rice

- ✓ 2 cups sushi rice rinsed
- ✓ 2 cups water
- ✓ 3/4 cup Rice vinegar
- ✓ 2 tablespoons sugar
- ✓ 2 teaspoons sea salt

Instructions

How to make Sushi Rice

1. Rinse the rice under water to wash away the excess starch. Place rice and water inside the instant pot or rice cooker and select rice sitting (instant pot) to cook for 10 minutes. Quick release the pressure.

2. Place rice on a baking sheet or a large skillet; using a spoon, break the rice.

3. Place rice vinegar, sugar, and salt into a small microwave-safe dish, and microwave for a few seconds to dissolve the sugar.

4. Pour the vinegar mixture over the rice and mix it well. Let it cool to room temperature.

How to make Shrimp Tempura Sushi Rolls

1. Follow the directions in the baking box to broil the shrimp. Wrap the sushi mat, then put the plastic wrap over it. Mix 1 nori sheet with rice and evenly spread it using either wet hands (wet your hands frequently to avoid adding too much rice) or a bowl of water (having a bowl of water next to you for strong rice spreading). Sprinkle 1 tablespoon of bonito.

2. Flip the nori on the other side and add shrimp, cucumber, and avocado slices. Tightly roll the sushi roll using a sushi mat.

3. After, wet a sharp knife with cold water and cut each sushi roll into 9 equal pieces. Drizzle Unagi Sushi Sauce (eel sauce) over the top and enjoy with soy sauce and spicy Mayo.

Shaggy Dog Roll Sushi

The Shaggy Dog Roll is a delicious sushi dish that can be easily made at home. It consists of cooked rice, sushi vinegar, nori seaweed, and fillings of your choice. This roll is perfect for those new to sushi making, as it is simple and easy to follow.

Prep Time 15 minutes | Cook Time 25 minutes | Total Time 40 minutes

Ingredients

Shaggy Dog Roll Ingredients

- ✓ 4 cups white sushi rice
- ✓ 3/4 cup sushi rice seasoning
- ✓ 7-8 sheets of Nori paper
- ✓ 2 packages of crab meat
- ✓ 6 tempura shrimp
- ✓ 3 avocados
- ✓ 8 sticks of imitation crab

Optional toppings:

- ✓ 3-4 tablespoons sesame seeds
- ✓ 2-3 teaspoons spicy Mayo
- ✓ 2-3 teaspoons teriyaki sauce
- ✓ 2 teaspoons Sriracha
- ✓ 2-3 teaspoons chopped green onion

Instructions

To prepare sushi rice:

1. Add rice to a large mixing bowl and fill it with enough water so that it covers most of the rice. Allow rice to absorb the water and chill until cloudy. Drain and rinse until the water is clear.

2. Prepare rice according to directions on the package or using a rice maker.

3. Once cooked, dump the rice into a large mixing bowl, add the sushi rice seasoning, and fold with a large wooden spoon to combine. Allow rice to cool for 25 minutes.

To make the roll:

1. While rice is cooling, cut the crab into 1/4 inches in strips and set it aside. Prep your avocado by removing it from the skin and cutting it into strips.

2. Scoop some rice into your hand, about the size of your palm and form into a softball. (When working with sushi rice, keeping a small water bowl nearby is helpful. Dip fingertips into the water before touching rice to keep it from sticking to hands. Do this as much as necessary while rolling your sushi).

3. Place the rice ball onto the top of the Nori sheet and spread it to all corners, covering evenly. Leave 1/2" along one edge of the nori sheet uncovered, as this will be how you seal your roll. Carefully flip so that the rice side faces down and the nori side faces up.

4. On top of your rice-covered nori sheet, layer outward across the middle of the 3 avocado slices, 5 tablespoons crab meat, 1 tempura shrimp (each cut in half, using one half as exterior of each avocado and crab meat)

5. Starting at the side of the nori covered with rice to the edge, tuck the edge in and begin to roll. When you've almost rolled it, dip your fingers in water and spread along the 1/2" of nori you left uncovered by rice. This dampened edge will adhere to the outside of the roll, sealing it as it dries.

6. Place a sushi mat over your roll and squeeze gently to tighten. Remove the sushi mat, rotate your roll 1/4 turn, then repeat the tightening process with the sushi mat. You can do this a few times if necessary.

Put it all together:

1. Place the crab sticks into a microwave-safe container and heat for about 12-17 seconds for every 3 pieces.

2. Remove crab sticks from the microwave and lay them on a cutting board. Cut the crab sticks in half and flatten them out on board. Place flattened crab sticks on top of the roll.

3. Place sushi mat over roll and crab, squeezing gently to tighten.

4. Using a sushi knife or chef's knife, cut the roll into 9-10 pieces.

5. Drizzle the salsa mayo mix and the green parts of scallions over the top as desired.

Lion King Sushi Roll

If you're a fan of The Lion King and sushi, then you'll love this Lion King sushi roll! It's a fun and easy way to show your love for both. This sushi roll is made with Salmon, avocado, and cucumber and is served with a sweet and savory sauce. It's the perfect meal for any Lion King fan!

Prep Time 15 minutes | Cook Time 15 minutes | Total Time 30 minutes

Ingredients

- ✓ 9 Oz Salmon
- ✓ 6 Tbsp Spicy Mayo
- ✓ 2 Tbsp Kewpie Mayo
- ✓ 3 Tbsp Unagi sauce
- ✓ 3 Tbsp tobiko/masago fish roe
- ✓ 3 Tbsp scallion - chop
- ✓ 3 sheets nori
- ✓ 3/4 medium avocado
- ✓ 1 mini/baby cucumber
- ✓ 3-5 pieces kani/surimi or 4 oz cooked crab meat
- ✓ 2 cups cooked & seasoned sushi rice
- ✓ 2-3 Tbsp Vinegar to wet your hand
- ✓ Pickled ginger as garnishment

Tools

- ✓ Bamboo rolling mat
- ✓ Plastic wrapper
- ✓ Foil

Instructions

Prep

1. Avocado - slice along its length
2. Cucumber - remove the seed, thinly slice along its length
3. Scallion - Finely chop
4. Salmon - thinly slice in a slant 47-degree angle (if possible)
5. Nori - fold and tear/cut if desire smaller bite-size roll
6. Crab - shred into a long thin strip and mix with 2 Tbsp mayonnaise

Roll

1. If you're new to making a sushi roll, read this post on how to roll inside out.
2. Start out by wrapping the rolling bamboo mat with a plastic wrapper.
3. Prepare a small bowl filled with 3 Tbsp of vinegar and water so that you can wet your hand to avoid stickiness.
4. Place the nori, smooth side down, onto the covered bamboo mat.
5. Wet your hand with the vinegar solution, then pluck some rice balls onto the nori.
6. Gently knead and spread the rice to the entire nori surface, do not mush.
7. Turn the nori upside down(i.e., the rice-covered side now facing down against the plastic).
8. Swoop a spoonful of the mayo crab onto the nori along its length, then add cucumber and avocado.
9. Now roll with the rolling mat; this will make a spicy inside-out California roll.
10. Arrange salmon sashimi on the California roll so that they will cover the entire length.

11. Gently roll the plastic wrap to shape them in place.

12. Let stand for 3 minutes before proceeding.

Bake

1. Preheat oven to 430F

2. Use a sharp knife to cut your rolls into pieces with the plastic still on.

3. Carefully unwrap each piece and arrange them on a prepared foil wrap, salmon side up.

4. Mix up spicy Mayo, unagi sauce, and 2 Tbsp tobiko.

5. Pour enough spicy Mayo and unagi sauce to cover the roll.

6. Fold the foil 5 sides around the roll to avoid sauce leaking.

7. Broil/bake for about 10 minutes, then pour the remaining sauce.

8. Bake for another 5 minutes until Mayo starts bubbling again.

9. Top with some tobiko and scallion and serve immediately with garnishment.

Dynamite Shrimp Sushi Jars

Sushi is a delicious Japanese dish that can be made at home with some simple ingredients. Dynamite shrimp sushi jars are a fun and easy way to enjoy sushi without all the fuss. These jars are perfect for a quick lunch or snack and also great for entertaining.

Prep Time 20 mins | Cook Time 20 mins | Total Time 40 mins

Ingredients

- ✓ 2 lb cooked shrimp (alternatively, you can use raw shrimp and boil with shells on for 2-3 min)
- ✓ 2 cups sliced red cabbage
- ✓ 2 cups diced cucumber
- ✓ 2 cups carrot matchsticks
- ✓ 2 packages of seaweed salad
- ✓ 2 sheets nori, cut into thin strips
- ✓ sesame seeds to serve
- ✓ Sriracha to serve
- ✓ soy sauce or tamari to serve

Sushi rice

- ✓ 2 cups water
- ✓ 2 cups cooked sushi rice (aka sticky rice)
- ✓ 2 tsp butter
- ✓ 2 tsp salt
- ✓ 3 tbsp rice wine vinegar
- ✓ 2 tbsp white sugar

Instructions

1. Follow the directions on the cooking package to make cooked sticky rice. Pour the sticky rice into a large serving bowl and mix together the butter, water, and salt until it achieves a creamy consistency. Stir in the cooked rice and a rice vinegar and sugar mixture and serve.

2. Assemble ingredients and add to jars, layering in the following order: soy sauce (to taste), shrimp, cucumber, red cabbage, carrots, seaweed salad, sushi rice, nori strips, sesame seeds, and Sriracha.

3. Jars keep in the fridge for up to 6 days. To serve, dump into a large bowl and enjoy!

Salmon Cucumber Sushi Boats

Sushi is a delicious and healthy Japanese dish that has become popular worldwide. Salmon cucumber sushi boats are a fun and easy way to make sushi at home. They are perfect for a light lunch or dinner and can be made ahead of time and refrigerated until ready to eat.

Total time: 25 MINUTES | Yield: 2 SERVING

Ingredients

- ✓ 2 salmon filets
- ✓ 1 tsp salt
- ✓ 3/4 tsp black pepper (omit for AIP)
- ✓ 2 tbsp avocado oil
- ✓ 2 tbsp coconut aminos
- ✓ 2 tsp lime juice
- ✓ 2 large cucumbers
- ✓ 3/4–1 cup cooked rice (sub-cooked cauliflower rice)
- ✓ 2 avocados, diced
- ✓ 3 tbsp spicy Mayo (use this for paleo or this for AIP)
- ✓ 2 tbsp green onion, chopped

Instructions

1. Remove the skin from the Salmon and pat dry. Slice the Salmon into small cubes and season with salt and pepper.

2. Microwave avocado oil in a wok over medium heat, then cook Salmon in it for about 5 minutes on either side. Pour Coconut Aminos and lime juice into the wok and bring the mixture up to a simmer. Liquefy the mixture by running a spatula around the bottom of the pan. Once you see the oil begin to cook, remove the Salmon and set it on a plate to absorb the remaining lime juice.

3. Wash the cucumber well, slice off the ends, and slice it in half vertically. Scoop out the inside until the cucumber is fully hollowed out.

4. Assemble the boats by filling them with rice, then topping them with Salmon, avocado, spicy Mayo, and green onion. Serve fresh.

Vegan Tofu "Katsu" Sushi Sandwiches and Rolls (Onigirazu and Maki)

When you think of sushi, the first thing that may come to mind is raw fish. However, sushi can be made with various ingredients, including vegetables and tofu. This vegan version of the Japanese dish is made with tofu katsu or crispy fried tofu. The tofu katsu is then rolled up in sushi rice and nori seaweed, just like traditional sushi. These vegan tofu katsu sushi sandwiches and rolls are perfect for a light lunch or snack.

Prep Time 45 mins | Rice Resting Time 1.30 hr | Total Time 2 hr 10 mins

Ingredients

- ✓ Whole nori sheets
- ✓ Prepared Japanese sushi rice (recipe below)

Tofu Filling (choose one!)

- ✓ Prepared tofu katsu, some sliced into strips for the rolls
- ✓ Other prepared tofu of choice (teriyaki tofu, black pepper tofu, smoked tofu, etc.)

Other Filling/Veggies (totally up to you!)

- ✓ Thinly sliced carrots
- ✓ Lettuce
- ✓ Pickled radish store-bought
- ✓ Pickled burdock root store-bought
- ✓ Homemade teriyaki sauce or store-bought
- ✓ Sesame seeds for sprinkling

Japanese Sushi Rice (Good for 2 serving)

- ✓ 2 cups uncooked Japanese rice or short grain rice
- ✓ 3/8 to 3/4 cup rice vinegar; this type of vinegar is essential (see notes)

✓ 2 tbsp cane sugar; feel free to adjust accordingly

✓ 1 tsp salt

Instructions

Japanese Sushi Rice

1. Wash the Japanese rice 3-5 times with water or until the water runs clear.

2. Cook in a rice cooker. (2 cups rice = 2 cups water)

3. While cooking, pour rice vinegar, sugar, and salt into a large wooden or ceramic bowl. Mix well.

4. Once the rice is cooked, add into the vinegar mixture and mix well. The hot rice will easily absorb the mixture.

5. Cover the rice with a damp towel. Refrigerate for at least 1 hour. Cover with a towel or cling wrap, then refrigerate.

Sushi Sandwiches (Onigirazu)

1. On a flat surface, place the nori sheet. Prepare a bowl of water to dip your fingers. This is to prevent the rice from sticking to your fingers.

2. Add a generous amount of sushi rice to make a square shape the same size as the tofu katsu or tofu of choice.

3. Add the lettuce and then the tofu.

4. Add other toppings of choice, all the same size as the tofu and rice. I used a mix of carrots and pickled radish.

5. Add another layer of rice and press down.

6. Fold each side of the nori sheet to the center while holding together the filling to ensure the sandwich will be held together well.

7. Fold the sheet up while tucking in the sides.

8. Flip over.

9. Wipe your knife with a damp towel to prevent the rice from sticking, then slice it in half.

10. Feel free to add some sesame seeds and teriyaki dressing if you like. If you want to pack these in the refrigerator, you can put them in a plastic wrap or seal them in a glass container to inhibit them from getting dry.

Sushi Rolls (Maki)

1. You can check out the video below on how to roll the maki.

   Prepare a bowl of water t dip your fingers. This is to prevent the rice from sticking to your fingers.

2. On a flat surface, place your bamboo mat. Place a sheet of nori.

3. Wet your hands. Thinly spread out the rice. Leave at least a 1/2" border at the other end of the nori sheet.

4. Add in the fillings of choice.

5. Fork up the nori sheet and compress it between both your hands. Create a few folds as you do so, then roll it up once more to both sides. Roll the finished sushi roll on the mat to compact it.

6. Slice the whole maki into 10 pieces with a sharp knife. Wipe your knife with a damp towel to prevent the rice from sticking.

Sushi Burrito (Sushirrito)

A new food trend is taking the internet and major cities by storm: the sushi burrito, or sushirrito. This delicious and convenient dish consists of all the best elements of a sushi roll wrapped up in a burrito-style package.

Sushirritos are perfect for on-the-go eating and can be customized with your favorite sushi fillings.

PREP TIME 25 minutes | TOTAL TIME 25 minutes

Ingredients

- ✓ 5 sheets Nori
- ✓ 2 batch prepared Sushi Rice
- ✓ 3/4 cup black sesame seeds (optional)
- ✓ 4 cups baby spinach, chopped
- ✓ 10 oz. teriyaki tempeh or tofu
- ✓ 2 avocados, sliced
- ✓ 3 carrots, peeled and julienned
- ✓ 3 Persian cucumbers, julienned
- ✓ 1 cup red beet & cabbage kraut (or raw purple cabbage)
- ✓ Soy sauce and wasabi, or Yum Yum Sauce for serving

Instructions

1. To make the single sushi burrito, lay down a sheet of nori on a piece of parchment paper or cutting board. Set out the ingredients for filling.

2. Top with about 1 cup of prepared sushi rice. Sushi rice is very sticky, so use wet hands to press evenly over the nori. Leave a 1/2-1 inch border at one edge to help adhere the burrito at the end. Sprinkle with about 1 teaspoon of sesame seeds if using.

3. Arrange the fillings over the rice, keeping them on the half farthest from the nori border.

4. Carefully lift the nearest nori border up and over the fillings, wrapping it very tightly like a burrito, taking care not to break the nori when doing so. It requires practice to cautiously roll this sushi burrito. If you overfill the sushi burrito, you can open it up and remove some.

5. Lightly wet the nori without the rice to help adhere the nori into a "burrito."

6. With a very sharp knife, cut the sushirrito in half. Enjoy immediately or wrap in parchment paper or foil and refrigerate for up to 4.30 hours.

Sushi Rice and California Rolls

Sushi rice is a type of short-grain white rice that is used to make sushi. It is also known as sushi-su or japonica rice. California rolls are sushi rolls made with avocado, cucumber, and crab meat.

Prep Time: 1.10 hour Cook Time: 25 minutes Total Time: 1 hour 25 minutes

Ingredients

Ingredients for Perfect Sushi Rice:

- ✓ 3 cups Japanese short or medium grain rice
- ✓ 3 cups cold water
- ✓ 6 Tbsp Sushi Vinegar

Make your own sushi vinegar by combining the following 3 ingredients and dissolving them together over low heat on the stove, then let the mixture cool:

- ✓ 5 Tbsp Rice vinegar
- ✓ 3 Tbsp sugar
- ✓ 3 tsp salt. I used sea salt

Ingredients for California Rolls:

- ✓ 1 lb Imitation crab meat, p.s. the "log" shaped crab meat is the easiest to work with
- ✓ 2 Avocados, ripe but still firm
- ✓ 1 medium cucumber, peeled and sliced into long julienne strips
- ✓ Toasted Nori Seaweed
- ✓ Toasted sesame seeds
- ✓ A rolling sushi mat, $3 at Cost Plus World Market. If you don't have a sushi mat, try using parchment paper instead.

For Dips/Sauces:

- ✓ Soy sauce, regular or low sodium

✓ Wasabi paste or wasabi powder

✓ For spicy Mayo: Mayonnaise, ~2 Tbsp and Sriracha hot chili sauce (~2 tsp) or to taste

Instructions

How to Cook Perfect Sushi Rice (Rice Maker and Stovetop versions): PS. Do not add salt while cooking rice.

1. Wash the rice with cold water until the water runs clear. Drain well. If you have a rice maker (way easier!), follow rice maker instructions and cook on the white rice setting, then skip to step #4

2. Pour drained rice into a thick saucepan and add 3 cups of cold water. Cover the pan tightly and put it over high heat to bring to a boil. Once it boils, reduce heat to medium and let simmer until all of the water is consumed (approximately 9 to 10 minutes). Do not uncover the pot during this time, but listen for the bubbling to cease.

3. Once you hear a faint hissing sound, reduce the heat to very low and cook another 6 min. Remove from the heat and let stand 20 min covered. This is the basic white rice eaten with Japanese meals.

4. Transfer the hot rice to a large bowl and break it up to get rid of all the hot clumps.

5. Let the rice cool down until it is just warm, then stir in your cooled sushi vinegar

Assembling your California Rolls:

1. Wrap your sushi mat in plastic wrap before using it (this makes it re-useable and you don't even have to wash it!).

2. Fold the pieces of nori in half to split them.

3. Toast your sesame seeds over medium heat, constantly stirring, until golden. Slice up your veggies.

4. Spread a generous handful of sushi rice onto the 1 sheet of nori. Use your WET FINGERTIPS (keep your hands wet to prevent

sticking) to spread the rice evenly over the entire surface of the nori.

5. Flip the rice-covered piece of nori over, so the rice is facing down (this way, your rice will be on the outside). Place your fillings across the center of your rice in the middle of the sheet (don't overfill, or the roll won't seal).

6. Pick out your roll and roll it backwards onto your mat, using your mat to stabilize the roll. Put your hands on the sides of the roll to make some pressure and make it a tight roll. Keep it so slack that it's hard still to cut it later. When you have cut it into tracklike strips, sprinkle them with sesame seed seasoned while you find it littered on your mat.

7. Run your sharp knife through a damp paper towel before slicing so the rice won't stick as much. Cut the roll in half, line the two halves up and slice even 1-inch rings. I have found that it slices easier when you slice quickly.

California Roll

A California roll is sushi, usually made with crab meat, avocado, and cucumber. It is one of the most popular types of sushi in the United States. California rolls are often served as an appetizer or as part of a sushi platter.

For 5 servings

Ingredients

- ✓ 3 cups sushi rice (490 g), cooked
- ✓ 3/4 cup seasoned rice vinegar (60 mL)
- ✓ 5 half sheets sushi grade nori
- ✓ 2 teaspoon sesame seed, optional
- ✓ 10 pieces of imitation crab
- ✓ 2 small cucumbers, cut into matchsticks
- ✓ 2 avocados, thinly sliced

Preparation

1. Season the sushi rice with the rice vinegar, fanning and stirring until room temperature.

2. On a rolling mat, place one sheet of nori with the rough side facing upwards.

3. Wet your hands, grab a handful of rice, and place it on the nori. Spread the rice evenly throughout the nori without mashing the rice down. Season rice with a pinch of sesame seeds; if using, then flip it over, so the nori is facing upwards.

4. Arrange, in a horizontal row 1 inch (2.5 cm) from the bottom, the crab, followed by a row of avocado and a row of cucumber.

5. Bending in front of the mat and snagging both nori and the mat, I place the mat on top of the filling so the unfilled space is adjacent to the bottom, squeezing down until I have a tight roll. Then I continue squeezing downward to keep the roll from changing.

6. Transfer the roll onto a cutting board. Rub a knife on a damp paper towel before slicing the roll into six equal portions.

Spicy Tuna Roll

A Spicy Tuna Roll is a sushi with raw tuna, rice, and nori (seaweed). It is usually rolled up in a cone shape and then topped with spicy sauce. There are many different ways to make a Spicy Tuna Roll. Still, the most common ingredients are tuna, rice, nori, and some spicy sauce.

Prep Time 35 mins | Total Time 35 mins

Ingredients

- ✓ 2 cups sushi rice (cooked and seasoned) (each roll requires 1 cup (155 g) sushi rice. 1.5 rice cooker cups (200 ml /180 g) make 380 g (15 oz, 2 cups) of cooked rice.)
- ✓ 5 oz sashimi-grade tuna
- ✓ 4 tsp sriracha sauce
- ✓ 1 tsp roasted sesame oil
- ✓ 3 green onions/scallions (cut into thin rounds)
- ✓ 2 sheets nori (dried laver seaweed) (each roll requires half sheet; cut in half crosswise)
- ✓ 3 Tbsp toasted white sesame seeds
- ✓ Homemade Spicy Mayo
- ✓ For Vinegar Water for Dipping Fingers (Tezu)
- ✓ 3/4 cup water (4 Tbsp)
- ✓ 3 tsp rice vinegar (unseasoned)

Instructions

1. Gather all the ingredients. Note: Cooking time is not include the time for making sushi rice. Please check the sushi rice recipe for a complete guide to making sushi rice. Important: Cover the sushi rice with a damp cloth to prevent it from drying. Cover your bamboo sushi mat with plastic.
2. Make vinegar water for dipping fingers (Tezu) by combining 3/4 cup (5 Tbsp) water and 3 tsp rice vinegar in a small bowl. Dipping your fingers prevents rice from sticking to them.
3. Cut the tuna into 1/4" (0.5 cm) cubes (or you can mince the tuna).
4. In a medium bowl, combine the tuna, Sriracha sauce, sesame oil, and some green onion (save some for topping).

5. Lay a sheet of half nori, shiny side down, on the bamboo mat. Wet your fingers in Tezu and spread 1 cup of the rice evenly onto the nori sheet. Sprinkle the rice with sesame seeds.

6. Turn the nori sheet over so that the rice side is facing down. Line the edge of the nori sheet at the bottom end of the bamboo mat. Place half of the tuna mixture at the bottom of the nori sheet.

7. Lay the divided into three parallel bands on the bamboo floor while keeping the shredded cabbage inside with your thumb. Takes hold of the bottom edge and continue rolling the cylinders forward by pulling the shredded cabbage close to your thumb.

8. With a very sharp knife, cut the roll in half and then cut each half into 4 pieces. Clean the knife with a damp cloth every few cuts. When you cut sushi rolls, dip your fingers in Tezu or cover the roll with plastic, so the rice won't stick to your hands.

9. Put a dollop of spicy Mayo on top of each sushi and garnish with the remaining green onion.

Shrimp Tempura Roll

In Japanese cuisine, tempura is a dish of deep-fried vegetables or seafood. Shrimp tempura is a popular variation in which shrimp are coated in a light batter and fried until crispy. This dish is often served with rice and vegetables, making for a well-rounded and satisfying meal. While it may take some time to prepare, shrimp tempura is well worth the effort!

Prep Time 30 minutes | Cook Time 20 minutes | Total Time 50 minutes

Ingredients

For the sushi rice:

- ✓ 3 cups uncooked sushi rice
- ✓ 3 cups water
- ✓ 3 tablespoons rice vinegar
- ✓ 3 tablespoons sugar
- ✓ 2 teaspoons salt

For the sushi rolls:

- ✓ 5 sheets of nori
- ✓ 9 pre-cooked tempura shrimp
- ✓ 9 strips of cucumber
- ✓ 9 slices of avocado
- ✓ 4 tablespoons black and/or white sesame seeds

Instructions

1. Place the rice into a colander and rinse until the water runs clear.
2. Add the rice and 3 cups of water into a medium saucepan over high heat. Bring to a boil, uncovered. Once it begins to boil, reduce the heat to low and cover. Cook for 20 minutes. Remove the pot from the heat and let stand, covered, for 15 minutes.
3. Combine the rice vinegar, sugar, and salt in a small bowl and heat in the microwave for 25-35 seconds. Transfer the rice to a large bowl and add the vinegar mixture. Fold thoroughly to combine. Allow the rice to cool to room temperature

4. Place one sheet of nori on a flat surface and press approximately 2/3-1 cup of rice across the surface of the nori, going all the way to the edges. This is easiest if your fingers are slightly damp.
5. Place a piece of plastic wrap over the rice-covered nori and invert it on top of a rolling sushi mat, so the seaweed side is up.
6. Place 3 shrimps, 3 strips of cucumber, and 3 slices of avocado along one side of the nori.
7. Pick up the edge of the rolling mat closest to the shrimp mixture and tightly roll up the sushi.
8. Press approximately 3 teaspoons of sesame seeds into the rice on the sushi roll.
9. Using a sharp knife, slice the sushi, then serve immediately.

Nigiri

Nigiri is a type of sushi that consists of a slice of raw fish placed on top of rice. It is one of the most popular types of sushi in Japan and can be found at almost any sushi restaurant. Nigiri is usually made with tuna, Salmon, or other types of seafood but can also be made with vegetables or tofu.

Prep Time 35 mins | Cook Time 35 mins

Ingredients

- ✓ 3 cups uncooked Japanese short grain rice
- ✓ 3/4 cup rice vinegar
- ✓ 3 Tablespoons cane sugar
- ✓ 1 teaspoon salt
- ✓ 1 lb. fresh, uncooked sushi-grade tuna
- ✓ 1 lb. fresh, uncooked sushi-grade salmon
- ✓ soy sauce, wasabi paste, and pickled ginger for garnish

Instructions

1. Cook rice according to package instructions, preferably in a rice cooker. While cooking, whisk the rice vinegar, sugar, and salt until the sugar and salt are completely dissolved. Once the rice is done cooking, place the rice in a large bowl, add the vinegar mixture to the hot rice, and toss. Set aside to let rice slightly cool.
2. After rice cools, cut the fish. Break the fish along the grain into slices that measure approximately 3 inches long, 1 inch wide, and 1/4 inches thick. Set them aside.
3. Form mounds of rice. Fill a small bowl with water, wet your hands, and place a small mound of rice that comfortably fits in your left hand (about 1 the size of your palm) when cupped. Keeping the left hand cupped, press down on the top of the mound with the long/inside surfaces of your right hand's pointer and middle fingers (together), gently forming the rice into a slightly more compact, structured mound. Don't squeeze the rice too tight. Set each mound aside and repeat until all rice has been used.
4. Combine the rice and fish to form pieces of nigiri. With your left palm facing up, lay one piece of fish horizontally across the base

of your fingers, and place one prepared mound of rice directly on top. Repeat the same motion as you did when forming the rice mound-- gently cupping your left hand and pressing down with the long side of your right hand's pointer and middle fingers, forming rice and fish together. Place pieces of nigiri on a large plate and serve immediately with soy sauce, wasabi paste, and pickled ginger.

Scattered Sushi (Chirashizushi)

Chirashizushi, or Scattered Sushi, is a type of sushi that is popular in Japan. It is made with rice, fish, and vegetables and is often served on special occasions. Chirashizushi is a fun and easy way to enjoy sushi and a great way to get your kids involved in the kitchen.

> Prep Time 25 mins | Cook Time 20 mins | Total Time 45 mins

Ingredients

- ✓ 5 cups cooked sushi rice (note 1)
- ✓ 9 fresh prawns/shrimps (medium size, note 2)
- ✓ 9 toothpicks
- ✓ 5 Simmered Shiitake Mushrooms, thinly sliced (note 3)
- ✓ 3 large eggs worth of Kinshi Tamago (shredded egg crepe, note 4)
- ✓ 7 slices of pickled lotus roots (note 7), cut into quarters (pie shape)
- ✓ 1 pack Japanese grilled eel (note 5)
- ✓ 55g/1.9oz sashimi salmon, finely diced (note 6)
- ✓ 45g/1.7oz snow peas

Instructions

Prepare Prawns

1. Remove heads and veins from the prawns.
2. Hold the prawn horizontally with the tail on the left (for a right-hander) and the belly facing down.
3. Put through a toothpick along the back between the shell and the flesh from the head end.
4. When the toothpick reaches halfway, point the tip downwards and push it further towards the tail, so the toothpick cuts through the flesh. This will prevent the prawn from curling when cooked.
5. Repeat for the remaining prawns.
6. Bring a small saucepan with water and a tablespoon of vinegar to a boil. Add the prawns and cook for a couple of minutes.
7. Drain, remove the toothpicks, let them cool and remove shells.
8. Butterfly the prawns by cutting the belly side from the head end to the tail, leaving the dorsal side of the flesh and skin intact.

9. Cut the butterflied prawns, perpendicular to the butterfly cut, into 3 similar size pieces (note 8).

Prepare Japanese Grilled Eel

1. Cut the grilled eel perpendicular to the backbone into 2cm - 3/4" wide pieces.
2. Cut each piece in half crosswise to make each piece almost square.

Prepare Snow Peas

1. Break the stem end of the snow pea gently and pull the tip towards the other end. The tough string that runs along the side comes off.
2. Pinch the other end, trim and pull the other side of the tough string (if you can) towards the stem end.
3. Place the snow peas in a microwave-safe bowl with a small amount of water, sprinkle a tiny amount of salt and cover with cling wrap. Cook for 1 minute.
4. Rinse under cold water to quickly cool them down. Pat dry with a paper towel.
5. Cut each snow pea pod diagonally into two pieces. If the pod is very large, cut it into three pieces diagonally so that you will have two ends and one diamond-shape piece.,

Assembly

1. Spread the sushi rice thinly on a large shallow plate.
2. Scatter simmered shiitake mushrooms over the rice.
3. Scatter kinshi tamago over so that the rice and mushrooms are mostly covered.
4. Scatter the lotus root pieces over the kinshi Tamago.
5. Place the prawn pieces on the red side up, randomly but evenly spaced.
6. Place the eel pieces with the skin side down, randomly but evenly spaced.
7. Make small balls with diced Salmon and place them where the large patch of yellow is.
8. Place snow peas randomly but evenly spaced.

Rainbow Roll Sushi Recipe

A rainbow roll is a type of sushi made with several different colors of fish. It is a very pretty dish to look at, and it is also delicious. This recipe is for a traditional rainbow roll, but you can add other ingredients to make it your own.

Prep Time 20 mins | Total Time 20 mins

Ingredients

- ✓ 1 cup Sushi Rice cooked
- ✓ 3/4 Nori Seaweed

For the Filling:

- ✓ 4 pieces Imitation Crab aka Surimi
- ✓ 4 slices Avocado
- ✓ 2 pieces of cucumber sliced lengthwise

For the Topping:

- ✓ 3 slices of Salmon, raw and fresh, rectangular
- ✓ 3 pieces of mango, not too soft, rectangular
- ✓ 3 slices of avocado, softer, rectangular

Instructions

1. Cut the nori sheet in half.
2. Place almost all the cooked rice over the nori sheet and reserve 3 Tablespoons. Spread rice over the nori sheet and press down, so the rice sticks to the seaweed.
3. Turn the rice on the nori sheet and sprinkle the remaining rice over the sheet. Extend the sheet of rice to about 1 2 inches or 1 centimeter horizontally and about 1 inch 2 centimeters vertically. Adhere to the sheet of rice.
4. Prep your filling ingredients. Keep sliced avocado and cucumber ready.
5. Place imitation crab pieces over the rice line, so the 3 pieces fit. Cut the center seafood stick if need be to make it fit properly.
6. Arrange the avocado and cucumber the same way.

7. Roll in sushi with the sushi mat with both hands and gradually press down while rolling in. That way, the sushi roll will be rolled tightly and won't fall apart after slicing it into pieces.

8. Peel the crust off your salmon and cut it into neat 0.1-inch 3-millimeter-thick slices. They should be rectangular in shape. Cut sections of mango and avocado into similar pieces.

9. Arrange Salmon, mango, and avocado slices topping over the sushi roll.

10. Place cling wrap over the rainbow roll and over the sushi mat. Press down so that the topping sticks to the cooked sushi rice.

11. Remove the cling wrap and mat. Cut the sushi roll into 8 equal-sized sushi pieces.

12. Serve up with soy, wasabi, and pickled Japanese ginger slices. Enjoy.

Temaki Sushi (Hand Roll)

Temaki Sushi is sushi rolled by hand into a cone shape. The word "temaki" means hand roll in Japanese. This type of sushi is usually made with nori, a type of seaweed, on the outside and filled with rice and fish on the inside. Temaki sushi is a popular dish in Japan and is often served at parties and special occasions.

Prep Time 15 mins | Total Time 15 mins

Ingredients

- ✓ 6 cups sushi rice (cooked and seasoned) (follow my recipe; 3 rice cooker cups of uncooked Japanese short-grain rice (550 ml, 3.5合, 480 g) yields roughly 6 U.S. cups or 1090 g of cooked rice; you must use short-grain Japanese rice to make sushi; otherwise, rice will fall apart.)
- ✓ 12 sheets nori (dried laver seaweed) (we use the half sheet for each roll)

Temaki Filling Ideas

- ✓ sashimi-grade fish of your choice (1 lb per person; Salmon, tuna, amberjack, yellowtail, fatty tuna, sea bream, salmon roe, uni, etc.)
- ✓ Japanese or Persian cucumbers
- ✓ shiso leaves (perilla/ooba)
- ✓ kaiware daikon radish sprouts
- ✓ takuan (pickled daikon radish)

Instructions

1. If your raw fish comes as a block, slice the raw fish into long sticks. Or you can ask a fishmonger at a Japanese grocery store to cut the raw fish for Temaki Sushi. They will cut fish into long sticks instead of sashimi-style cuts.
2. Right before you start eating, cut the nori in half (restaurant-style) or quarter (home-style; makes 45 taco-style rolls) and keep it in the bag as it becomes stale easily.
3. Prepare sushi rice, ingredients, and nori sheet (seaweed) at the table.

4. Before you start, ensure your hands are dry to keep nori dry and crispy. Place the seaweed on the palm of your hand (shiny side down) and put a thin layer of rice on the left third of nori. If you're using a 3/4 sheet of nori, put the rice and filling in the center and roll up the sides like a taco.
5. Place fillings (shiso leaf, cucumber, raw fish, and daikon radish sprouts) vertically across the middle of the rice.
6. Fold the bottom left corner of nori over and begin rolling into a cone shape.
7. Keep rolling until a cone shape is formed. Put a piece of rice in the bottom right corner to glue and close tightly. Continue with the other half of the nori.
8. Serve with pickled ginger, wasabi, and soy sauce as condiments.

Japanese Sashimi (Raw Fish)

Sashimi is a Japanese dish that consists of raw fish. It is typically served with rice and soy sauce. Sashimi is a popular dish in Japan and is also gaining popularity in other countries. There are many different types of sashimi, and the most common type is tuna.

Prep Time 15 minutes | Total Time 15 minutes

Ingredients

- ✓ 3/4 lb sashimi grade salmon
- ✓ 3/4 lb sashimi grade tuna or any other fresh fish you like
- ✓ 2 Tablespoons wasabi; you can get this ready-made in a tube or make your own with wasabi powder
- ✓ 3/4 lb shredded daikon radish
- ✓ 1.5 container pickled ginger
- ✓ soy sauce
- ✓ roe Optional

Instructions

1. Using a very sharp knife, cut the pieces of fish against the grain to about 3/4 slices or less.
2. Arrange the fish on a sushi tray and defile some daikon radish, some wasabi, and ginger slices. A common courtesy custom among broadcaster is a Japanese soy sauce container with a little dish for guests to mix used wasabi with sauce of the proper heat. Ginger is used to clean out the palate in between bites.

Temari Sushi

Look no further than Temari sushi if you're in the mood for a light, refreshing meal. This Japanese dish is made with vinegared rice and various toppings, all neatly rolled up in a ball. It's the perfect meal to enjoy on a warm day. Plus, it's so pretty to look at you'll be sure to impress your dinner guests.

Prep Time: 20 minutes | Cook Time: 0 minutes | Total Time: 50 minutes

Ingredients

- ✓ 5 cups sushi rice – visit my post on how to make sushi rice

Temari Sushi Toppings

- ✓ You can use whatever toppings you like for Temari sushi, but here are the ones I used for this recipe:
- ✓ Radishes, thinly sliced
- ✓ Avocado, sliced
- ✓ Carrot
- ✓ Cucumber, thinly sliced
- ✓ Scallions, finely chopped
- ✓ Shiso leaves
- ✓ Black and white sesame seeds
- ✓ Crab sticks
- ✓ Nori
- ✓ Sushi-grade salmon roe
- ✓ Sushi grade tuna
- ✓ Boiled Shrimp

Instructions

1. Grab a saran wrap and place about 2 ounces (about 3 tablespoons) of rice in the center. Seal and shape the rice into a ball. Squeeze tightly when making the ball but not so tight that the rice is being mashed.
2. Take the rice ball out of the saran wrap and place it on a plate. Cover with a damp towel or plastic wrap.
3. Repeat this step until all the rice is used.

4. Now that you have made your Temari sushi, it's time to add some fun touches like toppings and vegetable cutters. Create something attractive and colorful, and experiment with vegetable cutters for unique shapes.

5. When decorating Temari sushi, place the flat ingredients, such as shiso leaf, sliced cucumber, sliced tuna, and radishes, in saran wrap and top with a sushi ball. Wrap the plastic wrap around the Temari sushi and twist it to close. This helps the toppings adhere to the rice, preventing them from falling off.

6. Take the Temari sushi out of the plastic wrap, place it on a serving plate and finish decorating with toppings. Repeat until all the Temari sushi is decorated. Always cover the plate with a damp kitchen towel or plastic wrap to prevent the rice from drying.

7. Refrigerate for no more than 1.10 hours, as the texture of the rice will not be pleasant once it's hard.

Sushi Bowl Recipe

Sushi is a Japanese dish that traditionally consists of cooked rice, vinegar, fish, and vegetables. It is typically served rolled in nori (seaweed) and can be accompanied by soy sauce, pickled ginger, and wasabi. This sushi bowl recipe is a fun and easy way to enjoy all sushi flavors without all the rollings!

Prep Time 35 minutes | Cook Time 35 minutes | Total Time 1.10 hours

Ingredients

- ✓ 2 recipe sushi rice prepared according to recipe directions
- ✓ 3 tablespoons rice vinegar
- ✓ 2 teaspoons sugar
- ✓ 3 teaspoons toasted sesame oil
- ✓ salt to taste
- ✓ 2 cups cucumber thinly sliced
- ✓ 2 pounds sashimi grade seafood such as Salmon or tuna, can also use cooked shrimp or imitation crab
- ✓ 2 avocados peeled, pitted, and sliced
- ✓ 3 sheets of nori cut into strips
- ✓ 3 teaspoons sesame seeds
- ✓ 3/4 cup green onions
- ✓ 3/4 cup mayonnaise
- ✓ 3 tablespoons sriracha
- ✓ wasabi, pickled ginger, tobiko, and soy sauce as desired

Instructions

1. Divide the rice between four bowls.
2. Whisk together the rice vinegar, sugar, sesame oil, and salt in a small bowl. Add the cucumbers and toss to coat.
3. In a small bowl, whisk together the mayonnaise and Sriracha. You can toss your fish in the sauce at this point or drizzle it over everything at the end; it's your choice!
4. Arrange 3/4 of the seafood and avocado over each bowl. Spoon 3/4 of the cucumbers into each bowl.
5. Add the nori, sesame seeds, and green onions to each bowl.

6. Drizzle the mayonnaise mixture over each bowl if you haven't already tossed it with the fish. Serve with wasabi, tobiko, pickled ginger, and soy sauce as desired.

Sushi Burrito

A sushi burrito is a type of sushi that is wrapped in a seaweed wrapper and often includes rice, fish, and vegetables. It is a popular dish in many Japanese restaurants.

Prep Time 25 minutes | Cook Time 20 minutes

Ingredients

Sushi Rice

- ✓ 2 cups rice
- ✓ 4 cups water

Sushi Rice Seasoning

- ✓ 3 tablespoons sugar
- ✓ 2 teaspoons salt
- ✓ 4 tablespoons rice vinegar

Spicy Salmon Sushi Mixture

- ✓ 2 cups sockeye salmon skin removed and chopped into half an inch piece
- ✓ 3-4 Tablespoons Spicy Mayo
- ✓ 2 teaspoons Soy Sauce

Veggies:

- ✓ 1 cup spinach
- ✓ 2 carrots thinly sliced
- ✓ 4 avocados thinly sliced
- ✓ 1 cup purple cabbage sliced
- ✓ 4 scallions sliced

Assemble the Burrito:

- ✓ 15 Seaweed Sheets
- ✓ 1 cup bowl of water
- ✓ 3/4 cup salmon skin crisped in a skillet
- ✓ extra spicy Mayo

✓ extra soy sauce

Instructions

1. Start by making sushi rice. Rinse the rice under water in a sieve for just 3 minutes.
2. Bring the water to a boil and as soon it boils, add in the rice, lower the heat and covers the post until the rice has cooked. Usually, this takes around 18-20 minutes.
3. In the meantime, mix the sushi rice seasoning in a small glass bowl ad microwave it for 35 seconds to help dissolve all the salt and sugar in the vinegar.
4. Once the rice has cooked, place it in a large bowl and allow it to cool to room temperature. Add the seasoning mixture to the rice and mix well.
5. For the Spicy Salmon Sushi: Mix all the ingredients together.
6. To crisp the salmon skin: peel the skin off the salmon fillets. Preheat a skillet over high heat with a teaspoon of oil. Add the salmon skin and crisp for about 5 minutes on each side. Allow it to cool and it will crisp up some more! Crumble the crispy Salmon into bits for sprinkling over the sushi burrito.
7. Prepare the veggies.
8. Assemble the burrito:
9. Start with the seaweed sheets. You'll need two full-size nori seaweed sheets for one full burrito.
10. On a cutting board, brush the edges of one seaweed sheet with water and then add the other to stick together and become one large piece.
11. Wet your hands very well. This is crucial! Otherwise, the sushi will stick on your hands and be a mess!
12. Take the sushi rice and press it firmly over half of the seaweed sheets (so you'll be looking at a full sheet of sushi rice while the other full sheet is without).
13. Now start piling your burrito filling along the center of the rice, one ingredient at a time.
14. Make sure to load up the spicy salmon sushi mix!! You can use crab meat or cooked shrimp if you don't want raw fish here.
15. Roll up the seaweed like you would roll up a burrito, except you don't need to fold over the edges.

16. Brush the part of the seaweed that doesn't have the rice with a thin brush of water so it sticks to the roll as you go.
17. And there you have it!! Slice it in half or enjoy it as it!!
18. Once rolled out and sliced. Drizzle extra Spicy Mayo over the top and sprinkle the crunchy salmon skin roll bits.
19. Dip the sushi burrito in extra Spicy Mayo and soy sauce and enjoy!

Printed in Great Britain
by Amazon

18380626R00043